WORLD

MATERIALS

at the
PARK

By
William Anthony

BookLife
PUBLISHING

©2019
BookLife Publishing
King's Lynn
Norfolk PE30 4LS
All rights reserved.
Printed in Malaysia.

A catalogue record for this book
is available from the British Library.

ISBN: 978-1-78637-446-2

Written by:
William Anthony

Edited by:
Kirsty Holmes

Designed by:
Danielle Jones

CONTENTS

Words that look like <u>this</u> can be found in the glossary on page 24.

Have you ever thought about what things are made of? Everything at the park is made of something: wood, paper, plastic, glass... These things are called materials.

Everything in the park is made of materials!

All materials have <u>properties</u>. We can describe a material, such as how rough or smooth it is, using its properties. Let's have a look at the materials at the park.

Hard

Smooth

A MATERIAL PARK

Think about being at the park. What material do you think might be used to make this slide?

Slides are made from either metal or plastic. Metal is good because it is strong, but it can get too hot in the sun! That's why lots of slides are made from plastic instead.

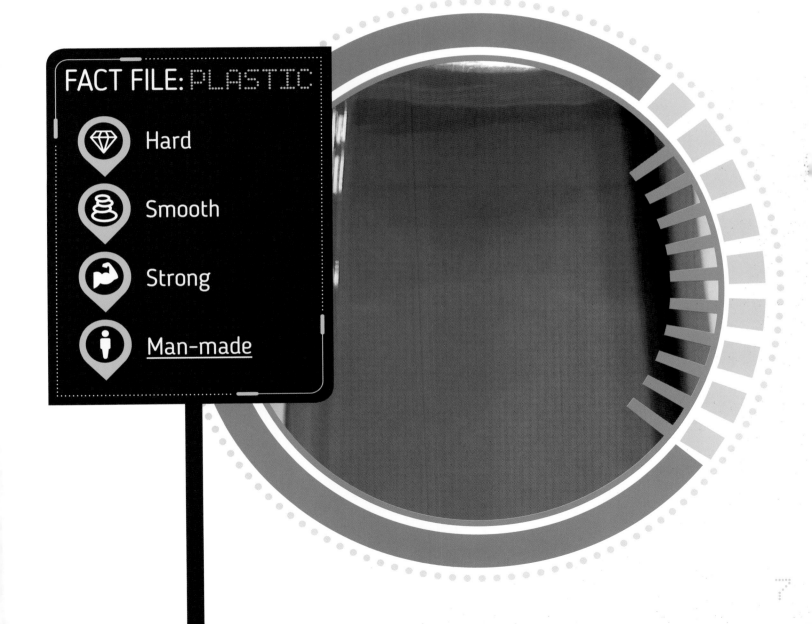

FACT FILE: PLASTIC

- Hard
- Smooth
- Strong
- Man-made

SWINGS

Does your park have normal swings or tyre swings? Although they look different, they normally have one material in common.

Tyre swings are made of big tyres from old wheels!

Swing seats and tyres are made from rubber. Natural rubber comes from rubber trees, but tyres are made from man-made rubber. Rubber is a good material for swings because it is strong and <u>durable</u> (say: jur-a-bul).

FACT FILE:
MAN-MADE RUBBER

 Smooth

Bouncy

Man-made

 Strong

ROUNDABOUTS

Have you ever spun round on a roundabout? It's hard to think about materials when you're dizzy, but what do you think the roundabout might be made of?

It's difficult to walk when you get off!

Roundabouts need to be strong and tough to carry lots of children, so they're made of steel. Steel is one of the strongest types of metal.

FACT FILE: STEEL

- ◈ Hard
- 💪 Strong
- ⚖ Heavy
- 🔗 Durable

CLIMBING NETS

Do you have a climbing net at your park? They are made from lots of pieces of rope tied together.

Rope

Rope is made out of lots of different <u>fibres</u> that have been twisted together. Rope is a good material for a climbing net because it is very strong, but also <u>flexible</u>.

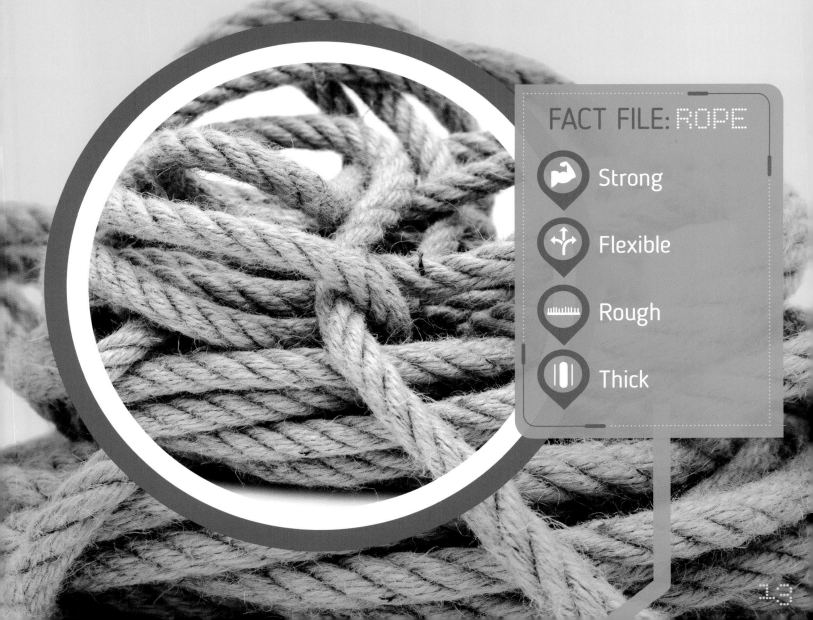

FACT FILE: ROPE

Strong

Flexible

Rough

Thick

BENCHES

After you are tired of playing, a good place to rest is the park bench. But what do you think it is made of?

The park bench is made of wood.

Wood comes from trees. It can be cut into lots of different shapes. Wood is hard and strong, so it can <u>support</u> people who sit on it.

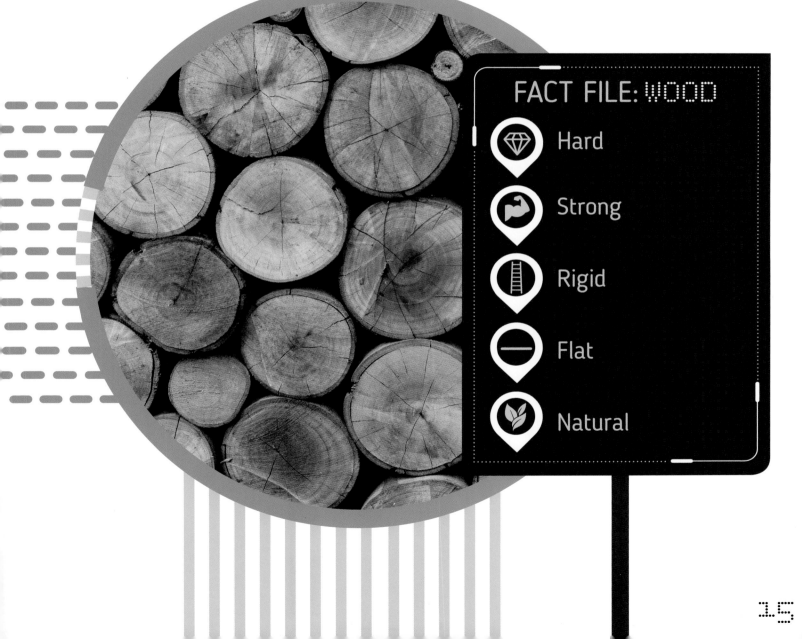

FACT FILE: WOOD

- Hard
- Strong
- Rigid
- Flat
- Natural

15

PICNIC BASKETS

When it's time for lunch, you might have a picnic at the park. What about your picnic basket – what do you think that is made from?

What's your favourite food to take on a picnic?

The picnic basket is made from wicker! Wicker is made by weaving different types of plant canes together. It is strong but light, making it easy to carry lots of food!

FACT FILE: WICKER

Natural

Strong

Light

PICNIC BLANKETS

You can't have your picnic without something to sit on! Picnic blankets feel soft and are light to carry. What material could they be made from?

Soft

Light

Picnic blankets are made from both cotton and PVC. Cotton is a natural material that is soft to sit on. PVC is a type of plastic and it stops you from getting a wet bottom when you sit down!

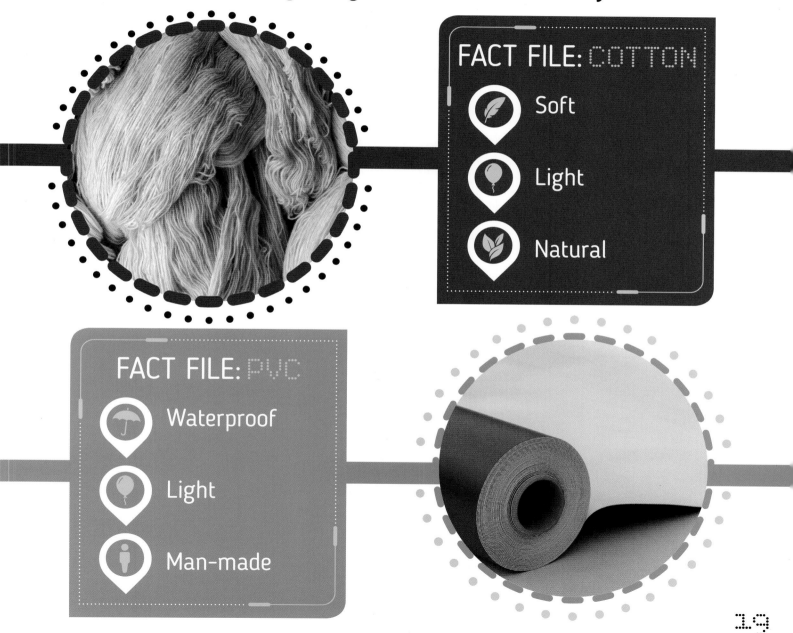

FACT FILE: COTTON

Soft

Light

Natural

FACT FILE: PVC

Waterproof

Light

Man-made

SANDPITS

Does your park have a sandpit? They are normally made from a wooden box filled with sand.

Sand can be used to make lots of other materials too.

Sand can be used to make glass, which is what the windows in your house are made from. It is made by heating sand up until it melts, and then shaping it.

FACT FILE: GLASS

 Hard

Strong

 Smooth

Transparent

MATERIAL MAGIC

Have you noticed that when you try to build something with dry sand, it doesn't work as well as wet sand? This is because sand changes properties when it is wet. It becomes stickier!

AT THE PARK

Can you find any materials at the park that have some of the following properties?

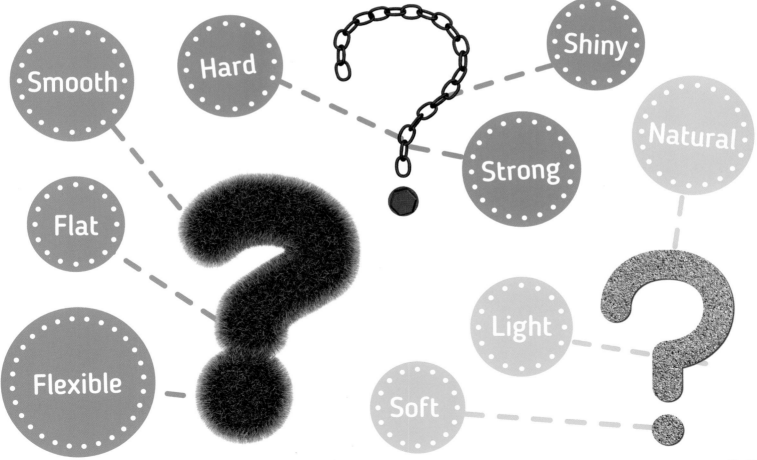

Smooth

Hard

Shiny

Flat

Strong

Natural

Flexible

Light

Soft

GLOSSARY

canes	hollow stems of some plants
durable	not easily broken or worn out
fibres	things that are like threads
flexible	easily bends
man-made	not natural: made by humans
natural	found in nature, not man-made
properties	ways of describing a material
support	to hold something and stay stable
transparent	can be seen through
weaving	passing threads over and under each other

INDEX